Career Skills
for the
New Economy

by

BRUCE TULGAN

HRD PRESS
Amherst, Massachusetts

Published by: HRD Press, Inc.
                 22 Amherst Road
                 Amherst, MA 01002
                 800-822-2801 (U.S. and Canada)
                 413-253-3488
                 413-253-3490 (fax)
                 http://www.hrdpress.com

ISBN: 0-87425-609-7

Cover design by Eileen Klockars
Editorial and production services by Mary George
Printed in Canada

❧ Dedication

This book is dedicated to my dear nieces and nephews:

Elisa Rose Tulgan
Joseph Perry Tulgan
Perry Elizabeth Ostheimer
Erin Rosalie Ostheimer
Frances Coates Applegate
Garret Elias Ostheimer

(Listed here from oldest to youngest)

CONTENTS

ACKNOWLEDGMENTS

FIRST AND FOREMOST, thank you to the many thousands of incredible people who have shared with me over the years the lessons of their own experiences in the workplace. I also want to thank all of the business leaders and managers who have expressed so much confidence in our work at RainmakerThinking and who have given me the opportunity to learn from the real management issues they deal with and solve on a daily basis.

To the tens of thousands who have attended my seminars, I once again say thanks for listening, for laughing, for sharing the wisdom of your experience, for pushing me with the really tough questions, for all of your kindness, and for continually teaching me.

Many thanks as well to Bob Carkhuff and his team at HRD Press. And thanks to all of my colleagues, present and past, at RainmakerThinking.

To my family and friends, I owe my very deep gratitude. And, as always, I reserve my utmost special thanks for my wife, best friend, and partner in all things, Debby Applegate.

INTRODUCTION

HOW DO YOU run your working life and career in the
midst of the most profound changes in the economy since
the Industrial Revolution? The old-fashioned career path
is dead. Now individuals are forced to reinvent success,
and most of us are making it up as we go along. No matter where you work, no matter what you do, you are on
your own. The only success you are going to achieve is
the success that you create for yourself.

This pocket guide is about creating success for yourself
in the new economy. It offers you best practices that
come directly from the *real strategies* of *real people* who
are *really succeeding* on their own terms. These practices
are among the most important findings of the ongoing
workplace-interview research conducted by Rainmaker-
Thinking since the mid 1990s.

The underlying assumption of *Career Skills for the New
Economy* is that, in the new economy, individuals will
have to be extremely good at fending for themselves if
they are to survive and succeed. The most successful
people will position themselves as free agents and sell
their skills and abilities on the open market. Even those

who work for the same employer for years on end will have to take responsibility for their own success and security.

The best practices outlined in this book are intended to give you an advantage when it comes to maximizing career opportunities, wherever and whenever you find those opportunities. Ultimately, this approach is quite simple:

◆ Make yourself as valuable as you possibly can, and your value will be well rewarded in the marketplace.

◆ Keep building yourself, and you will build the kind of success that is durable even in today's chaotic, rapidly changing world.

These two points constitute the bottom line. The best practices cover nine career-skills areas, which are introduced in the overview below and form the main body of the pocket guide.

OVERVIEW OF THE POCKET GUIDE

Chapter 1 briefly explains how the workplace of the future has evolved from the very different workplace of the past. It also clues you in on the four realities that are shaping change and details seven important factors of the new economy for you to keep in mind.

Chapters 2 through 10 each cover a series of best practices in a particular area:

➡ *How to Create Your Own Success.* Focus on the four key spheres of individual success—learning, relationships, work, and personal wellness—and set realistic goals in each sphere.

➡ *The Art of Managing Yourself.* Clarify who you really are, what really matters to you, what you want to achieve, and how you want to achieve it; figure out where you fit in any situation.

➡ *The Critical Thinking SQUAD.* Learn a simple method for critical thinking and problem solving that can be applied to the evaluation of almost any piece of information.

➡ *Become an Expert in Human Relations.* Follow eight simple rules for dealing with people, whatever the nature of your relationship with them.

➡ *Build Relationships with Valuable Decision-Makers.* Get beyond "networking for the sake of networking," and reach out to the decision-makers of value—*the ones who can really help you.* There are ten steps for you to follow; all of them require that you have actual business to transact—and that you have something valuable to offer in return.

➡ *Learn to Manage Your Boss.* If you follow these six guidelines, you will be able to help your manager *help you* succeed.

➡ *Get Good at Managing Others.* These six strategies will help you bring out the very best in others.

➡ *Adopt a Total Customer Service Mindset.* Everyone is your customer in the new economy, so focus on identifying opportunities to add value, selling your way into those challenges, delivering the value you promise, and always going the extra mile.

➡ *Success Happens One Moment at a Time.* Begin taking action right now.

Once you start practicing these career skills for the new economy, you will be at a strategic advantage when it comes to achieving success in your working life.

THE CALL FOR CAREER-SKILLS TRAINING

RainmakerThinking has brought many of these best practices to career counselors at colleges and universities throughout the world. Because the response has been so positive, and because so many people have asked for more resources to teach career skills, I have developed a training program to accompany this pocket guide. *Career Skills for the New Economy Seminar* will be the latest in our growing line of HRD Press books and training programs.

A FINAL NOTE

To help you get the most out of this material, I have included the following features:

- ◆ Clear and simple explanations of each career skill, based on real-workplace case studies

- ◆ Concrete action steps

- ◆ Exercises for productive brainstorming

- ◆ Worksheets for applying the ideas and action steps to the issues you are facing (or may face) in your own working life.

If the ideas and strategies in these pages help you improve your working life and add to your success, then I have succeeded with this pocket guide. Please let me know—I'd love to hear from you. Send me an e-mail at *brucet@rainmakerthinking.com*. Talk about your work at *www.winningthetalentwars.com*.

WELCOME TO THE
WORKPLACE OF THE FUTURE

WHEN THINKING ABOUT YOUR CAREER NOWADAYS, you need to be aware that we are living through the most profound changes in the economy since the Industrial Revolution. Technology, globalization, and the accelerating pace of change have yielded chaotic markets, fierce competition, and unpredictable resource needs.

In the late 1980s, business leaders and managers began responding to these factors by seeking much greater organizational flexibility. Reengineering increased speed and efficiency with improved systems and technology. Before long, companies in every industry were redesigning almost everything about the way work gets done. Work systems, some of which had been in place for decades, were dismantled and refashioned to improve flexibility, efficiency, and effectiveness.

As businesses reinvented work processes, they also eliminated layers of management, making way for today's fluid cross-trained teams, which tackle whatever work needs to be done whenever it needs to be done. Downsizing and restructuring made organizations leaner and more elastic by expanding their repertoire of staffing options; instead of having to rely solely on full-time, long-term employees, companies could also draw on temps, independent contractors, part-timers, and the like, and so staff up or down on an as-needed basis. That's why the fastest growing forms of work in the last ten years have been temporary work, leased work, outsourced work, consulting, and small to mid-size business entrepreneurship (fueled largely by the booms in temping, leasing, outsourcing, and consulting). Each of these forms of work lends flexibility to employment relationships.

In a relatively brief span of time, then, organizational response to economic change has virtually freed work from the confines of the old-fashioned job. It is no longer the norm for employees to go to work every day at the same company in the same building during the same hours to do the same tasks in the same position with the same responsibility in the same chain of command. Now the rule of thumb is, get the work done—whenever you can, wherever you can, however you can—whatever the work may be on any given day.

To compete in today's high-tech, fast-paced, knowledge-driven global economy, business organizations need to be flexible more than anything else. Because of that, the nature of work has been fundamentally reshaped and the relationship between employers and employees radically altered forever.

THE OLD-FASHIONED CAREER PATH

Throughout much of the twentieth century, until these profound changes took hold, the path to success for the typical individual was quite clear: you hitched your wagon to the star of an established employer, paid your dues, and climbed the company ladder for decades until you retired with a gold watch. Although some people did achieve success in other ways, in the workplace of the past this path was the "default presumption." It defined the social norm of success. And it was the path most people considered when thinking about their career possibilities.

In that workplace of the past, work was arranged in neat little packages. Why? Because this yielded what organizations needed: stability, continuity, and predictability, with longevity of employment serving as the solidifying force. You could expect your working life to be defined by a "job description" that would set boundaries around your tasks and responsibilities. It told you what you were supposed to do—and what was "not your job" and, therefore, not your problem. Most of your formal training occurred in school, before you entered the workforce. Once you got a job, you learned the specific things you needed to learn in order to do "your job." You worked in the same building every day and answered to one boss, probably the next guy up the company ladder. You did what your boss told you to do for about eight hours a day (sometimes a little more, sometimes a little less) and then you went home for dinner.

These careers were linear. You started with an "entry-level" job and moved along from one pay raise to the next, from one middle-management position to the next. If your boss got promoted, maybe you would get his job, and if you did get it, then you would probably keep it until he got promoted again and you could move up another rung of the ladder—and so on.

In that workplace, what mattered most was seniority. The longer you worked in a company, the more seniority you accumulated; and the more seniority you had, the more status, power, and salary you could expect. For those in the workforce of the past, it made a lot of sense to get a "good job" in a "good company" and stay put—pay the dues, climb the ladder, and become part of the club.

THE FOUR REALITIES SHAPING CHANGE

To see the future clearly, we need only look through the lens of these four realities:

1. ***Employers of every size in every industry must remain in a state of constant flux.*** Why? Because markets are chaotic (and will remain so) and therefore resource needs are unpredictable (and will remain so). To succeed in the new economy, organizations must be infinitely flexible.

2. ***Individuals must be able to fend for themselves.*** If established institutions must remain in a state of constant flux in order to survive, then individuals cannot rely on these institutions to be the anchors of their success and security. To survive and succeed, individuals must be self-reliant. That means you need to keep your options open at all times and be ready to adapt whenever necessary.

3. ***The information tidal wave grows every day, and there is no end in sight.*** Consequently, it is no longer possible to convince anybody that there is one way to think about or do anything. You and everybody else will be presented with nearly an infinite array of options at all times.

4. *Immediacy continues to accelerate.*
   Because the pace of change increases every day, the only relevant time frame is real time, *right now.* That means *just-in-time* is the new schedule for everything.

SEVEN FACTORS OF THE NEW ECONOMY

Here is a checklist of what's going on in the workplace of the future:

 ### 1. Reengineering

To maximize available technology, companies are continually redesigning the way work gets done. Work systems are refashioned time and again to improve flexibility, efficiency, and effectiveness. This means that the way tasks and responsibilities are getting done today may be wholly different from the way they will be getting done tomorrow. Don't dig in your heels; go with the constant change.

 ### 2. Restructuring

As organizations continually reinvent their work processes, they continually shuffle people around and assign more and more work to fluid cross-trained teams. Thus, even within organizations, people are in a state of constant motion. Even if you are assigned to a particular "department" or "team," you must be prepared to be pulled away and thrown onto another team at a moment's notice, and for only as long as you are needed.

 ### 3. Technology

Technology has shaped change throughout history, but today's technological advances are so rapid and fundamental that they transform tasks and responsibilities on a regular basis. They also blur work's traditional boundaries. Work that used to take a long time to do no longer does. Work that had to be done in a certain place no longer does. Work that required many people no longer does. Meanwhile, whole new categories of tasks and responsibilities routinely emerge that nobody knows how to do because they didn't exist before the new technology. Be the first person to figure out the "what" and the "how" of brand-new tasks and responsibilities when they emerge.

 ### 4. Knowledge-Work

There is steadily less "low-skill" work to do in the new economy. Because of advances in technology and business processes, more and more work requires more and more skill and knowledge. Be aware, though, that knowledge-work is not about what you do, but rather how you do it. To fit the definition of a knowledge-worker, you must leverage information, skill, and knowledge in every one of your tasks and responsibilities. That means two things: first, no matter where you work, no matter what you are doing, you must continually upgrade your skill and knowledge; second, in every task and responsibility, you have to identify the information resources and the skill and knowledge that you must leverage in order to make your work product more valuable.

 ### 5. Diversity

The workforce is becoming more and more diverse from every demographic angle, and the wide range of life experiences, perspectives, preferences, values, and styles of this diverse workforce is radically rewriting even the most basic expectations about ways of doing business. Don't expect to think, feel, or behave in terms of one "dominant" point of view. To succeed, you must be open to and supportive of other people's differences. You should also think about what makes you "different" from others and be proud of that and leverage that while also being sensitive to others.

6. Globalization

Technological advances in communication and transportation have removed one barrier after another to international trade and shared cultural influences. Multinational companies began blurring the boundaries decades ago. More recently, CNN brought a common news source to people at all ends of the globe. With the rise of the Internet, the doors have been blown off their hinges. Almost anyone today can buy from foreign suppliers, manufacturers, retailers, and wholesalers; sell to foreign companies and foreign consumers; tap into existing markets, open new markets, start up foreign ventures, and take over and reinvigorate existing business entities. If you're not thinking global, you might as well hide under your desk.

7. The Virtual Workplace

Few people need to go to work in a particular building during a particular set of hours anymore. Because of technological advances, most people can work nearly anywhere and anytime as long as they have a place to "plug in." Although working at a computer from a remote location is a solitary experience, such workers are not isolated but linked to a vast network of people and information through computer networks, the Internet, cell phones, and the like. In the virtual workplace, you may find yourself working alone most of the time, but you'll have access to seemingly infinite resources all the time. And you'll be able to reach practically anybody at any time, regardless of physical boundaries, and people will have access to you, as well.

IT'S ALL UP TO YOU

Employers today require flexible workers who are prepared to do whatever needs to be done. And that means continually upgrading skills, adapting to new conditions, assuming tasks and responsibilities in uncharted territory, working with one team today and another tomorrow, working eighty hours this week and twenty-five the next. No matter where you work, no matter what you do, don't hand over responsibility for your career to anyone else. The only way to succeed in the workplace of the future is to take charge of your career and assume one hundred percent responsibility for your own success.

How to Create
Your Own Success

HERE IS THE BOTTOM LINE: No matter where you work, no matter what you do, you are in business for yourself. You are the sole proprietor of your skills and abilities. That means you need to create your success on a daily basis by pursuing four key strategies:

1. Learn strategically and voraciously.

2. Build relationships with individuals who can help you.

3. Add value, no matter where you work or what you do.

4. Always keep yourself in balance.

This chapter focuses on these important strategies and will help you build a good foundation for using them.

LEARN STRATEGICALLY AND VORACIOUSLY

Right now, for nearly any subject, more information is produced in a single day than most of us could master in an entire lifetime. And the knowledge we do have becomes obsolete more rapidly than ever before. Meanwhile, work in the new economy is increasingly information- and knowledge-based, and so to succeed in that economy, a person must wield up-to-date marketable skills and knowledge.

There are two crucial dimensions to strategic learning in the new economy:

1. Building a wide repertoire of transferable skills
2. Becoming a knowledge-worker

1. Building Transferable Skills

Transferable skills are defined as skills that (a) are unlikely to become obsolete anytime soon, and (b) increase your value, no matter where you go or what you do. For example, skill in using a particular software package is not necessarily transferable because software becomes obsolete quickly and not all organizations rely on the same software. However, the ability to get up to speed easily on most new software packages (to learn them quickly and start using them effectively) *is* a transferable skill. Other examples of transferable skills include the ability to negotiate and fluency in foreign languages.

▷ Brainstorm

- **Think of other examples of transferable skills.**

- **What transferable skills do you currently have?**

- **What transferable skills would you like to add to your repertoire?**

2. Becoming a Knowledge-Worker

Leverage skill, knowledge, and wisdom in every project you undertake, every task you accomplish, and every responsibility you assume. Even if you are digging a ditch, you can leverage skill, knowledge, and wisdom:

- *What is the most effective technique for gripping the shovel? Striking the ground? Lifting the dirt?*

- *What kind of shovel should you use? What kind of gloves?*

- *What is the best physical posture? The best pace?*

Skill is the mastery of technique (gripping the shovel, striking the ground, lifting the dirt). *Knowledge* is the mastery of information (the best kind of shovel, gloves, posture, pace). *Wisdom,* the most complicated of the three, comes from an understanding of many perspectives (there is more than one "best" way to hold the shovel, strike the ground, lift the dirt; more than one "best" kind of shovel, gloves, posture, and pace). The wise person understands that the best way for one person may not be the best way for another; that the best way for one situation may not be the best way for another.

As long as you use skill, knowledge, and wisdom in your work, you are doing knowledge-work.

▶ Brainstorm

- Take a minute to clarify for yourself the meaning of skill, knowledge, and wisdom. Then list examples.

  Skill—Mastery of technique. Examples:

  Knowledge—Mastery of information. Examples:

  Wisdom—Understanding many perspectives. Examples:

- Think of the tasks/responsibilities you have that require skill, knowledge, and/or wisdom. List them. For each, identify the elements of skill, knowledge, and/or wisdom involved.

Task/Responsibility	Skill	Knowledge	Wisdom

▶

▶ Brainstorm

- Think of the tasks/responsibilities you have that do not require skill, knowledge, and/or wisdom. List them.

  TASKS/RESPONSIBILITIES:

- Re-evaluate the tasks/responsibilities you have just listed above. For each one, identify elements of skill, knowledge, and/or wisdom you can leverage to transform the tasks/responsibilities into knowledge-work.

Task/Responsibility	Skill	Knowledge	Wisdom

BUILD RELATIONSHIPS WITH INDIVIDUALS WHO CAN HELP YOU

The only reliable anchors you will have in today's fluid world are other people; therefore, this strategy is an essential one. Be sure to build firm loyalties with people you already know and trust. More difficult but just as necessary is building mutually advantageous relationships with individuals you *don't* already know and trust. How do you do that? One key is to always approach relationships in terms of what you have to offer others, rather than what you need or want from them.

 Brainstorm

- **Whom do you know and trust in your life right now? List those people in the space below.**

➤

▶ Brainstorm

● **What opportunities do you have right now to build relationships with new people?**

Make a list of people who are currently "available" to you (for example, at work, in school, in a community group, in your neighborhood, in your family life). To whom could you reach out to start building new relationships?

Also, take a moment to think about what you might be able to offer each person.

PEOPLE	WHAT YOU MIGHT HAVE TO OFFER

ADD VALUE, NO MATTER WHERE YOU WORK OR WHAT YOU DO

Prepare to be an entrepreneur, no matter what you do. You have to sell your way into every challenge, and, ultimately, the only thing you have to sell is your added value. So what is your "added value"?

There are five different ways to add value:

1. Get a lot of work done (accomplish tasks in a timely and competent manner or deliver an existing product or service).

2. Identify a problem that nobody else has identified.

3. Solve a problem that nobody else has solved.

4. Improve an existing service or product.

5. Invent a service or product.

By the way, don't underestimate number one—it is by far the most readily available way to add value (and often the most appreciated).

Remember: Wherever you go, sell your added value.

▶ Brainstorm

- **What are your current opportunities to add value?**

  — *Where/How can you get a lot of work done right now?*

  — *What problem can you identify that nobody else has identified?*

  — *What problem can you solve that no one has solved?*

  — *What existing service or product can you improve? How can you improve it?*

  — *What service or product can you invent?*

- **What challenges can you sell your way into right now?**

Always Keep Yourself in Balance

If you are in business for yourself (and you are), you are the employee and the manager; the main office and the factory; the producer, salesperson, and distributor. You are YOU, INC., and you had better take good care of yourself.

Especially important are the personal components of your mind, body, and spirit.

1. Your Mind

The key to a healthy mind is variety of input. Also, do not take yourself too seriously (relax), but do take a serious interest in other people, things, events, and issues. And learn to recognize feelings of anxiety so you can use anxiety without allowing it to paralyze you.

2. Your Body

The key to a healthy body is a solid routine that includes plenty of rest and daily exercise (stretching and walking are easy and very beneficial). Also, put healthy food and drink (especially water) into your body, and try to limit how much garbage (like cigarette smoke) you force your body to process.

3. Your Spirit

The key here is more problematic, but usually people with a healthy spirit believe in something that feeds their inner resources and imparts meaning. So believe in something—anything—and spend some time every day with your true beliefs.

Above all, remember the ultimate secret to a healthy mind, body, and spirit: *rebound.* When you slip up and drag yourself down for a day, a week, a month, or even more, forgive yourself, be patient, and get right back to healthy habits. What else is there to do?

▶ Brainstorm

YOUR MIND . . .

- **What are the main sources of input for your mind right now?**

- **How can you pursue a greater variety of input?**

  — *What new music, art, literature, or entertainment can you give your mind?*

  — *What new ideas can you give your mind?*

▶

▶ Brainstorm

— *What new teachers can you give your mind?*

— *What new experiences can you give your mind?*

YOUR BODY . . .

● **What is your physical routine right now?**

— *When do you sleep?*

— *What do you eat?*

— *What do you drink?*

— *How do you exercise?*

— *Other?*

YOUR SPIRIT . . .

● **How is your spiritual life right now?**

● **What do you believe?**

● **What do you want to believe?**

DO YOU HAVE A VISION FOR YOUR FUTURE?

I always hesitate to encourage people to create long-term visions of their future because long-term visions often turn into long-term goals, and today such goals have virtually no chance of ever materializing. How could they? Who knows where we'll be or what we'll be doing several years from now? The likelihood is that we'll be doing things that haven't even been thought of today.

Yet, it is still important not to let uncertainty hold you back. A long-term vision is like a mirage in the desert: You move toward the oasis perpetually, your destination always beyond reach; but you do keep moving toward *something.* The thing is, if you don't have a vision of your future, you can become mired in uncertainty, stay in one place for too long, and eventually sink into inertia.

It's better to move forward steadily toward an illusion than to stay in one place scratching your head and wondering what to do next. The things you learn on the way won't be an illusion, and they will serve you well whatever the future *does* hold.

Worksheet: SETTING GOALS FOR SUCCESS

1. Create a Vision for the Future

What does your life and career look like in ten years? Picture your ideal vision:

What have you learned? Are you an expert in a certain field? Are you well educated? Self-taught? Do people come to you for advice? Are you considered "the best" at something? Are you still practicing, learning, thinking, studying?

> **BRAINSTORM YOUR VISION:**

With whom have you built relationships? Are you closest to your family, friends, spouse/significant other? Who are your colleagues? Clients and customers? With whom do you do business? Who are your mentors? Whom do you mentor? Are you cultivating relationships with people you care about?

> **BRAINSTORM YOUR VISION:**

➤

> **WORKSHEET**

Where have you added value? Are you working for yourself, or someone else? As a professional? A volunteer? A valued team player? An entrepreneur? Have you discovered a problem, or solved a problem, that no one else has discovered or solved? Have you improved a product or service? Invented something? Are you still contributing to the world around you?

BRAINSTORM YOUR VISION:

Have you kept your life in balance? Do you have a gratifying home life? Are you close to those who matter to you? Have you lived your life with integrity? Are you proud of what you have done so far? Have you sought after your dreams? Are you healthy in mind, body, spirit? Do you exercise? Read? Meditate? Are you a person upon whom others can depend?

BRAINSTORM YOUR VISION:

➤

> **WORKSHEET**

2. Use Your Vision to Start Moving Forward

Now set goals for yourself. Drawing on your vision from step one, set at least one goal in each category below that you can likely achieve in the next 12 months.

LEARNING:

BUILDING RELATIONSHIPS:

ADDING VALUE:

MOVING YOUR LIFE TOWARD GREATER BALANCE:

3. Think About the Goals You Have Set

Review your goals. Think about them. Revise them as necessary. Finalize them.

REVISE & FINALIZE:

3

THE ART OF
MANAGING YOURSELF

IF YOU ARE GOING TO SUCCEED in the new economy, the
first thing you must be able to do is manage yourself. The
key to managing yourself can be found in the answers
to four simple questions:

1. Who are you?

2. What do you want to achieve?

3. How do you want to be as a person?

4. Where do you fit in each situation?

This chapter focuses on those questions and offers a
number of useful guidelines for arriving at your answers.
Included are brainstorming exercises that will help you
fine-tune your answers and develop the art of managing
yourself.

WHO ARE YOU?

Follow these guidelines:

1. Get in touch with your uniqueness.

2. Examine your priorities.

3. Grow.

1. Get in Touch with Your Uniqueness

What makes you different from everybody else? If you've always wondered where you fit in, then not fitting in with the crowd may turn out to be your special niche. Identify something in your background or experience that sets you apart.

- Is there something that qualifies you to better understand, connect with, or maximize a particular market?

- Is there something about your own unique perspective that lends itself to hard work, problem solving, creativity, or innovation?

- Exactly what is it that makes you special?

You have to get in touch with your uniqueness in order to leverage it in your working life and career.

▶ Brainstorm

- **Describe what makes you unique. Perhaps it's not one particular characteristic or trait, but rather your own combination of them.**

  List your most notable characteristics/traits in the space below.

Once you get in touch with your uniqueness, don't let it go. Your uniqueness is what you have that nobody else has. Leverage it.

2. Examine Your Priorities

What matters the most to you? The answer to this question is highly important because if your priorities are clear and you stay in touch with them, many decisions that would otherwise be tough will be quite easy for you.

For example, let's suppose your family means the most to you. What happens when you must choose between working all weekend and attending your child's birthday party? If your priorities are clear, that's a no-brainer. It's also a no-brainer if missing work would seriously threaten your job and thus your ability to support your family.

But what if missing work would be more a threat to your popularity at work than to your job? In such a case, you would have to be honest with yourself and get in touch with your priorities. What's more important to you—being popular at work or being there for your children? Again, a no-brainer.

Of course, you might try to figure out a way to get your work done *and* attend the party. What if you got up at 3 a.m., worked like a dog, and then joined the celebration? You wouldn't get much sleep, but what's more important to you—getting sleep this weekend or meeting your work obligations and being with your child? Another no-brainer.

You also might consider the possibility of "faking it," making it look like you were at work or stopping by the party to make an appearance. This option, too, should signal a priority alert: what's more important to you—being genuine, and truly meeting your obligations, or "looking good" to others, and getting away with doing less? Yet another no-brainer.

Again, if your priorities are clear and you keep those priorities in mind, choices like these will not be so difficult to make.

The next time somebody asks you to do something that you don't want to do but feel compelled to do, ask yourself:

Am I considering this because it really matters to me—though it may be difficult or inconvenient or interfere with other things I need to do—or because I want to be popular with this person?"

Or, the next time you find yourself procrastinating about something that you really need to get done, ask yourself:

Are all the things I keep doing more important than the things I really need to do? Do they matter more to me? Or are they just easier, more fun, or more convenient?

Brainstorm

- **Clarify your priorities. What things in your life matter the most to you?**

  Record your answer in the space below.

Once you clarify your priorities, make sure they come first in every decision you make from now on. Don't forget: Put your priorities first.

3. Grow

If you've ever studied weight training, you know that the way to build muscles is to push them beyond their limits, to the point at which the fibers actually tear, because the healing will make them grow stronger. That technique applies to more than just muscles.

We grow only when we push ourselves and keep pushing until we feel the pain; we then recover—only to push ourselves some more. To exceed our current level of ability or experience in any sphere, we have to move out of our comfort zone into the unknown. And in doing so, we increase the risk of making mistakes and getting hurt. That's why the key to growth is embracing the unknown, working through mistakes, and tolerating pain.

Of course, it is pointless to venture into the unknown without doing as much research and preparation as possible; to risk mistakes without a good backup plan; to welcome pain that signals injury. But don't turn common sense into an excuse for atrophy. And don't forget that as a living organism, you cannot remain static. Atrophy is the only alternative to growth.

So push yourself until you feel the pain. Recover. And then push yourself some more.

▶ Brainstorm

- Select an opportunity to grow that you have not yet tackled.

  OPPORTUNITY: _____

- What is holding you back?

  — *What unknowns are you afraid of encountering?*

  How can you research those unknowns and prepare to diminish them?

  — *What mistakes are you afraid of making?*

  How can you make a back-up plan for each of those possible mistakes?

  — *What pain are you afraid of experiencing?*

  How will you distinguish between the pain of injury and the pain of growth?

- Are you now ready to move forward and tackle this opportunity for growth? If not, why not?

WHAT DO YOU WANT TO ACHIEVE?

Follow these guidelines:

1. Start every endeavor with clear goals.
2. Hold yourself to strict deadlines.
3. Take action and keep moving forward.
4. Use your time wisely.
5. Fail, fail, fail, but never give up.

1. Start Every Endeavor with Clear Goals

Before you invest your time and energy in anything at all, clarify for yourself exactly what it is you are trying to accomplish. What is the tangible result you should be holding in your hands when you are done?

▶ Brainstorm

- **Think of something you're working on right now that is important to you. How clear is your goal? What tangible result are you aiming for?**

2. Hold Yourself to Strict Deadlines

Deadlines are the key to making a plan of action and managing your time effectively. The trick is to use deadlines every step of the way. Simply break up large goals and deadlines into smaller, more manageable pieces—intermediate goals and deadlines—thereby establishing benchmarks for your progress.

For example, if you need to achieve a particular goal by Wednesday, what needs to be done by Tuesday? Monday? Sunday? Saturday? If you know you need to achieve a particular goal by June 1, then what needs to be done by May 1? April 1? March 1? If you know you need to achieve a particular goal by 5 p.m., then what needs to be done by 4 p.m.? 3 p.m.? 2 p.m.?

Once you have a schedule of intermediate goals and deadlines, you're ready for the final planning step: making a list of concrete actions—essentially, a to-do list. As you tackle each concrete action and move toward each intermediate goal and deadline, you can monitor your effectiveness along the way. If you find yourself off schedule, you know you need to reassess your approach:

— *Are you taking the concrete actions you've planned?*

— *Are they taking longer than you thought? Or are you running across unexpected obstacles?*

— Do you need to revise the plan? Or to change something about your work habits?

▶ Brainstorm

- Think of a concrete goal you are currently trying to achieve. (It can be the goal you used in the previous brainstorming exercise). Set a realistic deadline for the goal. Then break that goal into intermediate goals and set a deadline for each.

Goal & Deadline	INTERMEDIATE	
	Goals	Deadlines

3. Take Action and Keep Moving Forward

Nothing gets done unless somebody does it. In this case, that somebody is *you.* If you have one hundred phone calls to make, you start with the first one, move on to the second, then the third, and so forth. Each call is a concrete action. But it's important to realize that each call also involves a series of concrete actions:

- Identify recipient and phone number.
- Clarify your purpose—why are you calling?
- Decide what you're going to say.
- Lift the receiver and hold in place.
- Dial the number.
- Wait and listen.
- Say hello and state who is calling.
- Conduct the conversation.
- Return the receiver to its cradle.

Every concrete action can be broken down into minute components, and each component is, itself, a concrete action.

Remember that fact whenever you get bogged down in the feeling that you're "not getting anything done." It's a good reality check, and can get you focused and back on track. If you break every task into its minute components and start tackling them one at a time, you will start moving forward.

▶ Brainstorm

- Don't forget: a list of concrete actions is a critical part of any plan. Go back to the intermediate goals you brainstormed in the previous exercise, and transfer them to the table below. Record the concrete actions needed to achieve each intermediate goal, and then estimate the length of time each action will take.

Intermediate Goal	Concrete Actions	Estimated Time

▶

> **Brainstorm**

- Now select one of the concrete actions you just listed, and break it down into its minute components. Next, estimate the length of time each component will take.

Concrete Action:

Components	Estimated Time

4. Use Your Time Wisely

There are 168 hours in a week. How do you use them? There are 1,440 minutes in a day. How do you use them? Most people waste countless minutes and hours without ever realizing it. How do you waste time? By filling it with activities that don't matter to you. What if you value just sitting around watching TV? I would argue that you are not wasting time if you know how much of it you are devoting to this activity and have a purpose for doing so. And that is the key: *Are you keeping track of your time and using it with a purpose?*

Worksheet: USING TIME WISELY

1. How do you spend your time?

How do you spend the 168 hours in a given week?

What does your typical day look like? (If some days are different from others, sketch each day separately or pick an average day.)

How much time do you spend . . .

- **SLEEPING?**

- **WORKING?**

- **WITH PEOPLE YOU CARE ABOUT?**

- **EATING?**

- **COMMUTING?**

- **EXERCISING?**

- **ON LEISURE ACTIVITIES?** (Be specific.)

- **OTHER?** (Be specific.)

➤

> **WORKSHEET**

2. Does this match your priorities?

How does your time allocation match up with the priorities you brainstormed earlier in this chapter?

3. How can you devote more time to priorities?

If you were to allocate your time according to your priorities, what would your typical day look like? How would you typically spend the 168 hours in a week?

TYPICAL DAY:

TYPICAL WEEK:

5. Fail, Fail, Fail, but Never Give Up

If you don't fail, chances are you will never succeed. So court failure. Be greedy with failure. Fail as much as you possibly can. You see, success may be preferable to failure, but statistically failure is far more likely. So turn the odds inside out.

Let's say you have a one percent chance of success. All that means is that you have to fail ninety-nine times for every one time you succeed. So you'd better hurry up and start failing. Look at it this way: You can fail only so many times—eventually, you will succeed, as long as you are not afraid to fail.

Most successful people will tell you that failure is a phenomenal learning experience—and it certainly is. But failure is also apt to derail success entirely if you don't welcome that experience and embrace failure itself. In learning to embrace failure, you develop the ability to *persevere*—a major key to success. With perseverance, you have the strength to bounce back from failure and keep trying; without it, you simply stop trying, and forfeit your chance to succeed in the end.

When things are going well, it's easy to "persevere." Real perseverance is the ability to fail, fail, fail (and even fail some more) but never give up.

▷ Brainstorm

- Think of a challenge you have attempted to meet and have failed at once, twice, three times, or more.

  CHALLENGE: _____

  — *Is this challenge important to you?*

  — *If you knew that you would eventually succeed, how many times would you be willing to fail?*

  — *How many times might you have to fail before you succeed?*

  — *Are you ready to give up this challenge, or would you rather fail until you succeed?*

- Think of a challenge that is important to you but that you have not yet attempted for fear of failure.

  CHALLENGE: _____

  — *If you knew that you would eventually succeed, how many times would you be willing to fail?*

  — *How many times might you have to fail before you succeed?*

  — *Are you ready to fail at this challenge until you succeed?*

HOW DO YOU WANT TO BE AS A PERSON?

Follow these guidelines:

1. Be high quality.
2. Be full of integrity.
3. Be adaptable.

1. Be High Quality

You are what you write, say, create, and do (in no particular order). No matter how grand your intentions or how generous and kind you may be as a person, others will know you by your words, actions, and creations.

So always hold yourself to a high standard:

- Think before you speak (and don't forget to rehearse).

- Outline before you write (and always do second and third drafts).

- Plan before you take action.

- Double- and triple- and *quadruple*-check anything and everything you do.

Then go for it. But don't let yourself be paralyzed by the myth of one hundred percent. You see, most people can effectively accomplish ninety-eight percent of the results of almost any undertaking in a rapid and efficient manner. If you ask me, ninety-eight percent is the highest standard of quality attainable by human beings. The two percent "error rate" is negligible.

I am *not* saying avoidable errors should be excused; clearly, that ninety-eight percent does not justify the kind of errors you can easily catch on double- and triple-checks. The two percent error rate I'm talking about is the central character in the myth proliferated by the procrastinators and failure-phobes of the world: the myth that they get nothing done because they are "perfectionists." Don't let that two percent keep you from executing the result, delivering it, and moving on to the next thing. That two percent is so relative, so open to debate, so intangible that it's just not worth agonizing over for even five minutes.

So, hold yourself to the highest standard attainable (ninety-eight percent), and go for it: Speak, write, create, and do.

▶ Brainstorm

- Think of a challenge you are now facing—a challenge that requires you to create something through your actions or to write or say something.

  CHALLENGE: _____

  — *What tangible result must you achieve?*

  — *What is the deadline for the first version of your response to this challenge?*

  — *Will that leave you time to double-, triple-, and quadruple-check?*

  — *Have you already started work on this challenge? If not, what are you waiting for?*

2. Be Full of Integrity

If your boss or customer wants you to lie, cheat, steal, or harm others, don't do it. Quit if necessary. Blow the whistle if you think it's appropriate. No matter what, don't get involved in unethical dealings. It's not worth any price. Be honest, and honest people will gravitate toward you.

But, let's face it, that's the easy part. How much judgment or effort is really required to reject downright dishonesty and corruption? The hard part is when integrity requires more than sitting on a high horse in judgment of others. Real integrity requires proactive behavior:

- Breaking your back to deliver, if necessary, when people are counting on you

- Helping others, even when nobody is there to give you credit

- Intervening when others are being treated unfairly

- Speaking out in support of causes that you believe in, even if those causes are unpopular

▷ **Brainstorm**

- **Think of an ethical dilemma you have recently faced or are now facing—one that required, or requires, proactive behavior on your part.**

  RECORD THE DETAILS OF THAT DILEMMA:

  _____

  _____

  _____

  _____ ▶

▶ Brainstorm

● What action did you take, or are you going to take?

IF THIS IS A DILEMMA FROM THE PAST:

— *Did you do the right thing? If so, how do you know it was the right thing? What was the consequence of your actions?*

— *Would you do anything different if faced with the same dilemma again? If so, what would you do? Why? What different consequences would you be looking for?*

IF THIS IS A CURRENT DILEMMA:

— *Are you planning to do the right thing? How do you know it's the right thing? What consequences do you expect from these actions? Are they the best ones?*

— *Is there anything you should do in a way different from how you're planning to do it?*

3. Be Adaptable

People who are too attached to the way things are have a hard time learning new skills, performing new tasks, doing old tasks in new ways, working with new machines, new managers, new co-workers, new customers, new rules, no rules. Usually, the greatest difficulty for such people is uncertainty—not knowing what will be (or won't be) just around the corner. Don't be one of these people. *Learn to love change.*

Master today's changes and tomorrow's uncertainty because things are going to keep changing, faster and faster, with or without you. When you realize your employer must constantly reengineer just to keep up with the pace of change, don't freak out. Be one of the few people willing to do whatever is needed, whenever it is needed, whether you already know how to do it or not; whether it is supposed to be "your job" or not; whether it is something you love to do or something you will have to tolerate for a few weeks or months.

Be flexible enough to go, on any given day, from one boss to another; from one team to another; from one organization to another; from one set of tasks to another. At any given time, you may be balancing three part-time "jobs," or moving from one short-term project to another, or working a day job and starting your own business, or doing all of those things and going to school at the same time. To move seamlessly between and among these different spheres every day, you need to be highly adaptable.

 Brainstorm

- **Think of a change that is in your immediate future.**

  <u>CHANGE:</u>

  — *What are all the likely effects of that change? In what ways will the change likely have an impact on you?*

  — *What have you done to prepare for the change?*

  — *What do you need to be doing to prepare for the change?*

WHERE DO YOU FIT IN EACH SITUATION?

Follow these guidelines:

1. Get good at evaluating context.
2. Play your role well before you build upon it.

1. Get Good at Evaluating Context

No matter who you are, what you want to achieve, or how you want to be as a person, your role in any given situation is determined in part by factors that have nothing to do with you. These are pre-existing, independent factors—factors that would be present even if you were not. These factors determine the *context* of any situation.

Context is "the big picture." To understand context, just imagine extreme contexts such as jail, war, famine, earthquakes, and floods. In any of these contexts, the possibilities are limited and so the scope of your potential role is limited. Whole sets of expectations, hopes, communications, and actions are excluded from the realm of the appropriate.

While it is relatively easy to be sensitive to extreme contexts, it is often very difficult to be sensitive to more subtle contexts, particularly if you're entering a situation that is new to you. Maybe you're attending your first weekly staff meeting, or joining a sales campaign or a research and development project; perhaps it's been a great year for profits, or there's been a corporate merger or budget shortfall. Such situations have a context that limits possibilities and the scope of your potential role. Whole sets of expectations, hopes, communications, and actions are excluded from the realm of the appropriate, but they are not necessarily obvious. Consequently, it's much harder to evaluate a subtle context, though no less important to do so in order to be successful.

Before you can figure out where you fit in the "context puzzle," you need to get a handle on the other pieces of that puzzle. How do you do that, especially if you are new to a situation? Begin by asking yourself the following questions:

- *Where am I? (What is this place?)*

- *What is going on here? (What is the mission of the group?)*

- *Why is everybody here? (What is at stake for the group and for each individual in the group?)*

- *When did everybody get here? (Not just today, but in the overall context.)*

- *Who are all these people? (What role does each person play?)*

- *How are they accustomed to doing things around here? (What is the standard operating procedure?)*

Once you have answered the questions above, you can ask yourself where you fit in this picture:

- *Why am I here?*

- *What is at stake for me?*

- *When did I get here?*

- *What is my appropriate role in relation to the other people in the group?*

- *What is my appropriate role in relation to the mission?*

- *Who am I in this context?*

2. Play Your Role Well before You Build upon It

Context doesn't have to slow you down indefinitely, but it certainly does limit your role, and for quite some time, if you have entered a new situation. Unless you properly evaluate the context of the situation and figure out where you fit, you will never have an opportunity to build on your role.

To play your role well in any context, you have to be able to determine the following:

- *What expectations and hopes about the situation are reasonable for you to have?*

- *What communications are reasonable?*

- *What actions are reasonable?*

Once you are actually playing your role well, the most productive ways to build on that role will become apparent over time.

▶ Brainstorm

- **Think of a new situation you are currently entering, or a new situation you have recently entered.**

  SITUATION: _____

- **Now figure out where you fit in the picture:**

  — *What are the big factors shaping the context of this situation?*

  ▶

Brainstorm

— *What is the mission of the group?*

— *Who are the other people and what is at stake for them?*

— *Where do you fit?*

  • *When did you get there?*

  • *What is at stake for you?*

  • *What is your appropriate role?*

  • *What do you need to do to play that role very well?*

THE CRITICAL THINKING SQUAD

CRITICAL THINKING is as much a habit as a skill. It has nothing to do with criticizing, disparaging, or finding fault. Rather, critical thinking involves differentiating between reliable and unreliable information, carefully weighing the strengths of conflicting views, and making reasoned judgments.

Critical thinkers do not leap to conclusions—they take the time to consider possibilities and do not become too attached to one point of view. They do not latch onto one solution—they know that most solutions are temporary and can be improved over time on the strength of new data. Critical thinkers are both open to the views of others and supremely independent in their own judgments.

The next time you catch yourself jumping to conclusions about a situation, stop and take the time to practice critical thinking. Suspend your judgment and question your assumptions; ask yourself, "What are all the logical possibilities *[who, what, when, where, how, and why?]* that my assumptions exclude?" Then check your facts. What do you really know about the situation? What is your source, and is it a good source? Is there a better source? What facts do you need to gather to make a better decision?

If you get in the habit of thinking critically, you will handle every situation more professionally, interact more effectively with people, make better decisions, and be able to resolve—at least provisionally—almost any problem. Such results make critical thinking the ultimate transferable skill. And unlike today's hot technical skills, it will never become obsolete.

To become a critical thinker, try the five-step SQUAD approach:

---

1. **S**uspend judgment.

2. **Q**uestion assumptions.

3. **U**ncover the facts.

4. **A**nalyze your information.

5. **D**ecide on your next step.

SUSPEND JUDGMENT

When you are presented with information—whether it's in the form of a question or an answer, a problem or a solution, raw data or artistic interpretation—simply pause and look at the information. Don't leap to conclusions. Don't take anything for granted. Don't believe in the content of that information, and don't doubt it, either—just pause for a moment and see what you're dealing with.

QUESTION ASSUMPTIONS

Once you have looked at the information, start asking yourself the hard questions: Do I have a clear picture in my head of the situation I am facing? What parts of the picture seem the clearest? Are those clear parts actually untested assumptions? How can I test those assumptions?

You need to question every single assumption: How do I know that? What is my source of information? Is that a reliable source? Is there another source? Does it fit with common sense? Does it fit with everything else I know? Am I sure? How sure am I?

The point of such interrogation is to figure out what you definitely *don't know* so you can be clear on what facts you need to uncover.

UNCOVER THE FACTS

The best guide to use is still the old standard:

> *Who? What? When? Where? How? Why?*

But remember, the key to successfully uncovering the facts of any situation is Step 2 above. Before you can uncover the facts, you have to know which facts need to be uncovered.

ANALYZE YOUR INFORMATION

Any sound analysis begins with a clear goal—an optimal outcome. You cannot analyze in a vacuum; you must analyze in terms of the particular results you are trying to achieve, whether you're focusing on a question, an answer, a problem, or a solution. It's also important to keep in mind the full range of results that constitute your goal: an answer may be very good in terms of one particular result, but very bad in terms of another.

If you analyze through the lens of what you are trying to achieve, you will be able to maintain your clarity and move forward.

DECIDE ON YOUR NEXT STEP

The key to making a decision is to link the decision to the next step it requires. Are you prepared to take that step? You haven't really decided anything unless you're ready to take *concrete action.*

**Remember this five-step approach
through its acronym:**

SQUAD

Now use the following worksheet to try out the critical thinking SQUAD on a piece of information you must evaluate, such as a question or an answer, a problem or a solution.

Worksheet: CRITICAL THINKING SQUAD

Directions: Choose a piece of information to evaluate; then apply the rules of the critical thinking SQUAD.

Information to evaluate:

• SUSPEND JUDGMENT
Stop, look, and listen. Then go on to . . .

• QUESTION ASSUMPTIONS
What don't you know? What facts must you uncover?

➤

> **WORKSHEET**

- ## UNCOVER THE FACTS
  Who? What? When? Where? Why? How?

- ## ANALYZE YOUR INFORMATION
  What is the goal through which you're going to analyze?
  What is the best course of action in terms of that goal?

- ## DECIDE ON YOUR NEXT STEP
  What is your next step? Define that step in terms of concrete action.

BECOME AN EXPERT IN HUMAN RELATIONS

THE ABILITY TO RELATE WELL TO PEOPLE has always been important, but in the new economy, this ability is more important than ever before. Remember, other people are your only anchors in today's fluid world. Everyone may be in constant motion, but human relations can be built and sustained, and they constitute a vital element of success.

Here are eight rules of human relations by which to live and work:

1. **Be a model of trust.**

2. **Remove your ego.**

3. **Listen carefully.**

4. **Empathize with people.**

5. Exhibit respect and kindness.

6. Speak up and make yourself understood.

7. Be a motivator.

8. Celebrate the success of others.

Let's take a closer look.

 ## BE A MODEL OF TRUST

Take personal responsibility for everything you say and do, hold yourself accountable, and never fall back on excuses when you make a mistake—instead, apologize and make every effort to fix the mistake.

 ## REMOVE YOUR EGO

Don't take yourself too seriously, but always take your obligations seriously. Extend personal vulnerability, but never undermine your credibility. Be honest and open.

 ## LISTEN CAREFULLY

Never interrupt when someone is speaking, and don't let your mind wander. Stay focused on what the other person is saying. When it's your turn to speak, first ask open-ended questions such as "What do you mean?" or "What would be a good example of that?" Listen carefully to the answers. Then, to ensure you understand what the person has said, ask specific, clarifying questions such as "Do you mean *[clearly say what you think the person means]*?" or "Are you saying *[clearly say what you think the other person is saying]*?" When you feel confident you understand, don't change the subject; instead, respond directly to what has been said.

 ## EMPATHIZE WITH PEOPLE

Try to imagine yourself in the other person's position. Ask yourself what thoughts and feelings you might have if you were in that position. Then behave in a way and say the kinds of things that you would appreciate under the same circumstances.

 ## EXHIBIT RESPECT AND KINDNESS

Take courtesy the extra mile. If you think the person is pressed for time, be brief. If you think something might be wrong, ask if there is anything you can do to help (but don't be pushy). Never share observations that might be insulting, and never hesitate to share a compliment.

6 SPEAK UP AND MAKE YOURSELF UNDERSTOOD

If you don't say what's on your mind, you'll have virtually no chance of connecting with people, getting them to share your interests, influencing their thoughts, or persuading them to do things your way. Of course, sometimes it helps to hold back for a quiet moment and clarify for yourself what really is on your mind. If it's something that ought to be shared, take an extra moment to decide which words and actions would most effectively get your message across.

 7 BE A MOTIVATOR

Visualize positive results. Be enthusiastic and share your positive vision. Never speak of a problem unless you have thought of at least one potential solution.

 8 CELEBRATE THE SUCCESS OF OTHERS

Always give people credit for their achievements, no matter how small those achievements might be. And go out of your way to catch people doing things right.

Now try out
the following exercise.

▶ Brainstorm

- Choose a person whom you value.

  VALUED PERSON:
  _____

- Evaluate your relationship as honestly as you
  can in terms of the eight rules of human relations.

    — _Are you a model of trust in this relationship?_

    — _What role does your ego play?_

    — _How well do you listen?_

    — _Do you empathize with this person's situation?_

    — _Do you treat this person with kindness and respect?_

    — _Do you speak up and make yourself understood?_

    — _Do you help to motivate this person to pursue his
      or her goals?_

    — _When this person succeeds, are you thrilled?_

- What can you do to improve your relationship with
  this person?

6

Build Relationships with Valuable Decision-Makers

Nearly everyone knows that building relationships with decision-makers is critical to success. "Networking" is something every ambitious person is always trying to do nowadays. The problem is, a lot of people out there are networking just for the sake of networking—and doing nothing but wasting much of their own time and the time of other busy people.

Don't bother networking with people unless you have a *very specific reason* for doing so—some real business to transact. This is especially important if you want to start building a relationship with someone you don't know; you need a reason for reaching out to that person. And it makes no sense to fabricate a reason—if you do that, then any relationship you might build will be disingenuous. Instead, wait until you have something genuine to talk about—best of all, something genuine *to offer.* Then you can honestly reach out to the person and approach the relationship with complete confidence.

When you are ready for networking, take the following ten steps:

---

1. **Clarify exactly what you have to offer.**

2. **Make sure the decision-maker is "right" for the transaction you have in mind.**

3. **Do some research before making contact.**

4. **Use a mutual connection.**

5. **Make your communications interesting and useful.**

6. **Turn every contact into a multiple contact.**

7. **Identify and win over gatekeepers.**

8. **Get the attention of the decision-maker by proving yourself.**

9. **Become Ms. or Mr. Follow-Up.**

10. **Routinely update contact information.**

In this chapter, we'll take a close look at each of these steps.

CLARIFY EXACTLY WHAT YOU HAVE TO OFFER

Even if your main concern is to get something out of the relationship, focus on what you bring to the table. This is possible, no matter what you might want or need. For instance, let's say you want lessons from someone. Instead of thinking "I want someone to teach me," reframe the situation: "I want to offer myself as a student." If you wish to teach, don't ask for students; rather, offer your skills and knowledge. Instead of asking to be introduced, offer someone the chance to introduce you. Instead of asking people to meet with each other, offer to bring people together. And so on.

MAKE SURE THE DECISION-MAKER IS "RIGHT" FOR THE TRANSACTION

Every person is a decision-maker by virtue of free will. But different people have decision-making authority in different spheres. You need to identify the decision-makers who have the authority to act on what you are offering, who can engage in the transaction you propose. If you want the service manager in a car dealership to sell you a car, that manager is not going to do it, no matter what you say; although he or she will be glad to make arrangements to have your car fixed. If you want to buy a car, you need to talk to a salesperson. Likewise, if you are selling a car, you need to talk to the party who will make the ultimate decision about whether to buy it. The same is true of any transaction. Make sure you are talking to the person who has the authority to make the decisions that will move you toward your goal.

DO SOME RESEARCH BEFORE MAKING CONTACT

Before reaching out to make a new contact of any kind, do a little research (or a lot) about the people you are trying to reach, their organization, and the work they do. Do you know anyone who is already familiar with those people or their organization or at least their industry? Maybe that person could answer some questions for you. Are there any relevant articles or books you could read? Maybe the people you want to contact have published material that you could find and read. Do they have homepages? Does the company have a website you could check out? Maybe there's a different organization, a professional association, or a government agency that could answer some of your questions over the phone. Or, you could call the office of one of those people before launching your contacts, speak with the person's assistant or co-worker without identifying yourself, and ask a lot of questions. You'd be amazed at how much you can find out.

USE A MUTUAL CONNECTION

Compare two situations: (1) I contact you out of the blue; (2) I contact you and tell you that I know your friend (or your uncle or your boss or your sister or your customer or your former teammate or anyone else you know). In the second situation, I carry a lot more weight with you. Why? Because how you treat me may have implications for other relationships which matter to you; for the simple reason that there is a person out there in the world whom we both know and who matters to you.

First rule of mutual connections: Make sure there is a positive relationship between the decision-maker you are trying to reach and your mutual connection. Imagine this: I contact you and tell you that I know your old teacher (the one you most despised in high school) or your uncle (the one who always pinched you and called you names) or someone you went to college with (the one who dumped you after your second date). Sometimes it's better not to mention mutual connections, so always check. Once you've confirmed that your connection is positive, you can go on to the second rule.

Second rule of mutual connections: Don't ask your mutual connection to make the introduction for you, or you'll be paralyzed. You won't be able to go ahead and introduce yourself—you'll have to wait until your connection gets around to introducing you. That may or may not happen, and even if it does, it's not likely to happen very soon. Moreover, you may be asking your connection to do something that, for whatever reason, he or she is not comfortable with (although don't expect your connection to tell you that). You may be asking more than you realize.

Instead, explain that you are planning to reach out to the person you want to contact. Ask the connection for advice; ask questions about the person, his or her work, the best way to reach the person, the status of your connection's relationship with the person. Then, simply ask if you can use the connection's name when you get in touch with the person. By following this rule, you're actually doing your mutual connection a favor: giving him or her the chance to help two people—both you and the person you want to reach—without having to do anything. You also maintain control over the process. Once you have a name to use, you're ready to follow the next rule.

Third rule of mutual connections: Use the connection's name shamelessly in your attempts to communicate with the decision-maker. For example, format your letters, faxes, and e-mails like this:

Date

Ms. Person You Are Trying to Contact
99 Contact Drive
Contact City, State 0000

RE: Letter from a mutual friend of Ms. Mutual Friend

Dear Ms. Contact:

[BODY OF LETTER]

Sincerely,
You

cc. Ms. Mutual Friend

Then send copies of every communication to your mutual connection. They might get tossed out, but by keeping your connection in the loop, you will be showing respect and recognizing the person's help. The decision-maker will also be more conscientious in dealing with you, for he or she will feel a greater sense of accountability about the relationship.

MAKE YOUR COMMUNICATIONS INTERESTING AND USEFUL

Demonstrate your value by making the materials you send appealing and useful. Send an article you think might be of interest, or one that mentions the decision-maker or you. Go one step further—write an article about a subject associated with the decision-maker, get it published somewhere, and send that along. Or just send a copy of the unpublished article. Here are some other ideas:

— *Do a little research, and dig up a useful piece of information to share.*

— *Paint a picture.*

— *Put together a spreadsheet.*

— *Send charts and graphs.*

— *Send a ten-minute infomercial.*

— *Direct the decision-maker to your personal homepage.*

— *Create a new logo for the person's business, or a prototype of the new product you are*

*inventing, or a life-size poster of yourself
holding out your resume.*

You'll think of something. Just make certain whatever
you do is in good taste.

TURN EVERY CONTACT INTO A MULTIPLE CONTACT

One of the most difficult things about reaching out to a
new person and trying to form a relationship is getting
on that person's radar screen—getting noticed. It takes
three to five contacts to get the average person to remember your name. If you are dealing with an extremely
busy person, it takes five to seven contacts. How do you
achieve multiple contacts without calling over and over
and over again and seeming like a pest? Simple—turn
every new contact into a multiple contact.

- ◆ Never *just* call and leave voice-mail at work.

- ◆ Never *just* leave a message on the answering
  machine at home.

- ◆ Never *just* overnight-mail a package to the office.

- ◆ Never *just* send a personal letter to the home
  address.

◆ Never *just* fax a note.

◆ Never *just* send an e-mail.

If you really want to make an impression, use all six methods of contact *simultaneously.* It takes more time and effort, but that's one reason to do it—you can be sure it's not what everyone else is doing. I promise, you will get on the radar screen (like an incoming missile attack!). As long as you do all the contacts at once, you will not seem like a pest. But you will seem very thorough.

A Word of Caution: Imagine going to all that trouble, getting on the radar screen, and then having nothing to say other than "No big deal, I just wanted to 'network' with you." If you go to all that trouble to get noticed by someone new, don't waste it.

IDENTIFY AND WIN OVER GATEKEEPERS

Even if you do everything right, the decision-maker may never even know you exist. Why? Gatekeepers. Many of the people you want to reach will be insulated from the outside world by assistants who carefully guard their time and attention. These assistants screen voice-mail, e-mail, paper mail, faxes, overnight packages, and any other communication directed at their bosses. That makes gatekeepers very powerful. And they have a strong personal incentive for keeping other ambitious people away from their bosses—who needs more competition? No matter how many times you call, write, fax, e-mail, and overnight, if the gatekeeper doesn't want you to get through, you probably won't.

But gatekeepers are people too. And if you want their help, you have to recognize them as individuals and take the time to build relationships with them.

First, identify the real gatekeeper by asking good questions: "Do you check Ms. Jones's voice-mail, or does she check it herself?"; "Do you keep Mr. Smith's schedule, or does he keep it himself?"; "If I send Ms. Jones a fax, would you be the person who would see it first?"

Second, once you have identified the real gatekeeper, treat that person with the same measure of respect and deference you would accord the decision-maker you are trying to reach. Teach the gatekeeper your name by using multiple contacts addressed directly to the gatekeeper: send a letter, voice-mail, fax, and e-mail, all at the same time, thanking the gatekeeper for taking the time to talk with you. Don't even mention the decision-maker in this round of communication.

Third, follow up with a phone call to see if the gatekeeper remembers you. If so, then it's time to ask the gatekeeper to raise the gate and let you in: "What would be the best way to get a fax directly to Ms. Jones?"; "How could I make sure that Mr. Smith will get my letter?" When you win over the gatekeeper, you will get past the gate.

GET ATTENTION BY PROVING YOURSELF

Once you get on the radar screen, you need to prove you're more than just a blip—getting noticed is not enough. How do you get decision-makers to stop and pay attention to you? By making it clear that you are offering to add value: "This is exactly *[what, where, when, why, how]* I am offering to add value." Of course, if you sell it, be prepared to deliver.

Another way to get attention is to set up a series of commitments with concrete deadlines and then keep the commitments, thus building an instant track record of reliability. These commitments can be minor—"I'll call you on Thursday at 10 a.m.," or "I'll look into that and get back to you by Friday"—but they must be specific and you must complete them as promised.

For the best strategy, commit to making a concrete proposal by a certain deadline and then deliver. If your first proposal is rejected, don't give up. Maybe the decision-maker will suggest an approach to revising the proposal. If so, then revise away. Keep proving yourself over and over again. Eventually, it will pay off.

BECOME MS. OR MR. FOLLOW-UP

Once you get the ball rolling, don't be the one to let it drop. Always follow up.

◆ If the relationship is hot (you just submitted a proposal), then your follow-ups should be frequent (once a week).

◆ If the relationship isn't going anywhere right away (the decision-maker said, "I'll get back to you if I'm interested"), then your follow-ups should be less frequent (every other month).

◆ If you aren't sure how the relationship is going, simply ask, "When is the best time for me to follow up next?"

If the response is "Get lost," don't call back.

If the response is "Why don't you call me in about a month," confirm a specific date and time and say you're writing the appointment on your calendar.

If the response is "You don't have to follow up; I'll call you in a few weeks," let the person know that if you haven't heard from him or her by a certain date, you will make sure to follow up.

Bear in mind, the more relationships you try to build, the more follow-ups you will have to make, and sometimes they will be scheduled months in advance. That means you need a system for keeping track of your follow-ups, so you won't forget them.

No system of this type is ideal. Keeping a calendar or schedule is effective, but you must check it every day. There is plenty of scheduling software that will give you a reminder automatically if you have an appointment scheduled, but you must learn the software and keep your computer on. You could simply keep a running list in your pocket, as many people do; but you must remember to update it. Whatever you do, just don't drop the ball.

 **STEP 10**

ROUTINELY UPDATE CONTACT INFORMATION

It is essential to keep contact information up-to-date, including information on how others can contact you.

People move around a lot these days, so it takes a little more effort to stay in touch. You'll need to maintain good records of the contact information for those with whom you're building relationships. Whether you use database software or an old-fashioned notebook, use your contact information (mail and e-mail addresses, phone and fax numbers) at least twice a year, so you can verify which information remains current and update information as it changes.

Also, make sure that your own current contact information is always available to people who want to stay in touch with you. If you are really on the move, think about getting a post-office box or voice-message service in addition to your e-mail address. Whenever you do move and your contact information changes, let everyone in your contact universe know at least twice. Send a post-card, leave a voice-mail, send a fax, *and* send an e-mail. Twice.

Now try out
the following worksheet.

Use the next worksheet to make a plan for reaching out to a decision-maker who can help you.

Worksheet: PLANNING TO REACH OUT

Directions: Choose a decision-maker who can help you; then follow the ten planning steps outlined below.

Who is the decision-maker?
(Note: You may need to revisit this question after Step 1 and 3.)

The decision-maker is . . .

1. Clarify what you have to offer.

2. Is this the right decision-maker?

Does this person have the authority to act on what you are offering? How do you know? You may have to do some research before you know for sure (see next step).

3. Do some research.

Research may be needed not only for the big picture but also to complete many of the remaining steps.

➤

> **WORKSHEET**

4. Do you have a mutual connection?

Who is it? You need to contact this person before you can use him or her as the connection.

Mutual connection:

---

5. What will you put in your communication?

How can you convey in an interesting and useful way what you have to offer?

Remember, you'll have to prepare several versions of the communication, with the same content but in a form appropriate to the medium.

For overnight delivery packages, you can include additional materials, such as samples of your work.

For telephone and e-mail messages, you must be very clear and concise.

For fax messages, you can use more words, but you still must get to the point quickly and make that point clearly.

Content:

> **WORKSHEET**

6. How will you contact the decision-maker?

You'll need contact information in advance for each method of communication.

Means:

7. Who is the gatekeeper?

Gatekeeper and contact information:

8. How are you going to prove yourself?

How will you prove you're more than a blip on the radar screen?

What set of simple commitments can you make?

(continued)

Commitments & Deadlines:

▶

► WORKSHEET

8. How are you going to prove yourself? (cont.)

What realistic dead-lines can you set for those commitments?

Commitments & Deadlines:

9. How will you follow up on your first contact?

How will you keep track of your follow-up schedule?

10. Do you have an information-update method?

You need a database or notebook for keeping up-to-date contact information. And you need a plan for getting your current contact information to others whenever it changes. How are you going to do that?

LEARN TO MANAGE
YOUR BOSS

YOUR MOST VALUABLE CAREER CAPITAL is your time, labor, and creativity. Whenever you are working, you are investing that capital. Maximize your investment. Pursue your work goals in a way that allows you to learn and grow; to build new skills and perform diverse tasks; to achieve tangible results and collect proof of your value in the workplace; to receive recognition, credit, and rewards; to maintain balance between your working life and home life; and to build relationships with people who can help you.

Work closely with good managers. Make the most of the learning opportunities they provide. Get them to help you formulate ambitious goals and determine realistic deadlines. Pay close attention to the feedback they give you, and appreciate the recognition, credit, and rewards they provide. *Never* stop earning the responsibility, creative freedom, and flexibility they want to provide for you.

The best managers are leaders, role models, teachers, coaches, and mentors—people who go to bat for anyone who works hard for them. You will never forget them, and they will never forget you. In fact, they may become some of the best friends you will ever have.

Bad managers, however, are a whole different story. No matter how miserable they may be, you cannot let them stand in your way. Remember, your boss is only your boss for today—tomorrow, he or she could be your customer, your supplier, teammate, subordinate, friend, adversary, teacher, student, spouse, in-law, or somebody you never see again. The hierarchy of your relationship is temporary. If your manager is getting in your way, you must take control of the situation.

To help your manager help you succeed, follow these six guidelines:

---

1. **Help your manager delegate effectively.**

2. **Get the feedback you need.**

3. **Set specific learning objectives, and get your manager's support.**

4. Always put requests in the form of a proposal.

5. Disentangle the micromanager.

6. Never accept abusive behavior from a manager.

HELP YOUR MANAGER DELEGATE EFFECTIVELY

With every assignment, ask up front for a concrete goal (a clear statement of the tangible results expected of you), a specific deadline, and all the related guidelines and parameters. Talk with your manager about the details of the assignment until you understand exactly where your responsibility begins and ends. Give that information back to your manager, stating it clearly, and then restate it to double-check your understanding.

Use the following tool
to help your boss delegate.

This tool will help you and your manager successfully work through the delegation process.

Worksheet: DELEGATING RESPONSIBILITY

Directions: Record a concrete goal (results expected),
specific deadline, and guidelines and parameters.

GOAL/ RESULTS	DEADLINE	GUIDELINES & PARAMETERS

Insist on specific deadlines, no matter how small or how large the goal of the assignment. If the result is too minuscule to justify a deadline, then your manager is not delegating enough responsibility. If the result is too large to fit a realistic deadline, then it is not sufficiently concrete. By insisting on clear deadlines, you will force your manager to clarify the assignment in question.

Once you have ownership of a concrete goal, a specific deadline, and all of the guidelines and parameters, use the assignment as your proving ground: Deliver and go the extra mile.

The following worksheet
will help you create a plan of action.

Complete this worksheet by employing some of the self-management techniques you learned in Chapter 3.

The worksheet is also an aid to delegation, for it can highlight any weaknesses in the set goal, overall deadline, and guidelines and parameters.

Worksheet: PLAN OF ACTION

Step 1

For each larger result you own, set intermediate goals and corresponding deadlines. For example, if you are going to deliver a report by June 1, what do you need to do by May 1? April 1? March 1? And so on.

LARGER RESULT:

INTERMEDIATE DEADLINES	INTERMEDIATE RESULTS
	➤

> **WORKSHEET**

Step 2

Review your list of intermediate goals and deadlines, and break down each goal and deadline into a list of concrete actions. Start taking action right away.

INTERMEDIATE DEADLINE	INTERMEDIATE RESULT	CONCRETE ACTIONS

GET THE FEEDBACK YOU NEED

You will probably get six- and/or twelve-month reviews
in most jobs, but those reviews usually feel few and far
between. And when they come, they often don't give
you the kind of accurate, specific, and timely feedback
you need to keep moving in the right direction.

The best kind of feedback you can get is day-to-day
performance coaching from a manager you trust and
respect. If you are not getting that from your manager,
you need to give it to yourself. Here's a good method:

1. When you accomplish a goal, note the achieve-
    ment in your calendar (or similar organizer).

2. Detail what you did well, so you can repeat the
    success.

3. Now take a moment to evaluate.

    — *Are there any ways to improve how you
    accomplished the goal?*

    — *Are there any obvious errors?*

    — *What can you do next time to achieve a
    higher level of quality?*

    — *Can you get it done smarter? Faster? More
    efficiently? More effectively?*

> *— What skill development might you pursue in
> order to do a better job next time?*

GUIDELINE 3

*SET SPECIFIC LEARNING OBJECTIVES, AND
GET YOUR MANAGER'S SUPPORT*

Make a list of every task and responsibility for which you
are accountable, and use this list to brainstorm some
specific job-related learning objectives. What skills
should you be practicing? What knowledge should you
be mastering? What wisdom should you be acquiring?
Go to your manager with this list and ask what resources
might be available to help you undertake some of your
learning goals.

GUIDELINE 4

*ALWAYS PUT REQUESTS IN THE FORM OF A
PROPOSAL*

Don't make requests lightly and they won't be taken
lightly. Always include in any proposal (big or small) the
following information:

◆ The benefit of what you are proposing to the
   organization and/or to your boss

◆ How it can be accomplished with minimum cost and little chance of something going wrong

◆ The resources you need, and where you think they can be obtained

◆ The potential problems, and the measures you propose to avoid those problems

◆ How you will solve the problems if they occur

◆ What role you foresee for yourself in this proposal

◆ The timeline for the proposal

Follow these guidelines whether you are proposing a major project or proposing that you take a day off. Regardless of how big or how small your request, make your proposal strong.

GUIDELINE 5

DISENTANGLE THE MICROMANAGER

Always set a day and time for a "next meeting" with your manager. If the manager tries to get tangled up in your work, take this simple approach:

1. Remind the manager of the assignment you are working on (the tangible results and your

specific deadline) and show your plan from
Guideline 1.

2. If your manager persists in trying to micromanage,
   remind him or her of the meeting you already
   have scheduled to review progress on the
   assignment.

It may take time for you to establish an appropriate
distance between you and your manager, but if you are
patient, this approach will usually give you some space.

NEVER ACCEPT ABUSIVE BEHAVIOR FROM A MANAGER

A manager who is intimidating, mean, or otherwise
abusive has psychological problems. When faced with
such a manager, you must remember, first and foremost,
that those problems are *the manager's,* not yours.

How do you deal with an abusive manager?

1. Document every instance of abuse and every
   solution you have attempted to end the abuse.
   Keep a notepad for your documentation, and be
   highly specific. Include dates, times, names,
   and concrete examples.

2. Seek support among your colleagues (and family and friends) while trying to avoid your abusive boss.

3. Once you have compiled a decent record of the abuse, report the behavior to senior management.

Although an experience like this is unpleasant, try to remember that, in the long run, you are helping this individual as well as yourself. The hope is that the manager will come to terms with the problems behind the abuse, resolve them, and develop into someone who can succeed and help others, like you, succeed too.

GET GOOD AT
MANAGING OTHERS

ONE OF THE MOST VALUABLE SKILLS you can possibly have
is the ability to get the best work out of the best people
on a consistent basis—the ability to manage effectively.
There is a good chance that sometime soon you will find
yourself in a position of supervisory responsibility. If you
are *not* good at it, you will find this to be a tremendously
frustrating experience. If you *are* good at it, you'll have
a chance to increase your productive capacity dramati-
cally by leveraging the time and energy of other people.

Be sure to follow these six guidelines:

1. **Empower people through effective
   delegation.**

2. **Make sure people can meet their assigned
   goals.**

3. Make sure people have the resources they need, and anticipate obstacles to the successful completion of goals.

4. Coach people by using *FAST Feedback*™.

5. Reward good performance and nothing else.

6. Never be abusive.

GUIDELINE 1

EMPOWER PEOPLE THROUGH EFFECTIVE DELEGATION

As we saw in Chapter 7, effective delegation involves assigning concrete goals and specific deadlines and clarifying all guidelines and parameters. Make sure that both you and the person you are managing are absolutely clear on what is expected. Talk about the details of the assignment until the person understands exactly where his or her responsibility begins and ends. Ask the person to state the details for you, and then ask for the details again in order to double-check understanding.

You can employ the "Delegating Responsibility" tool introduced in Chapter 7 as an aid for empowering people effectively. The tool is repeated here for ease of use.

Worksheet: DELEGATING RESPONSIBILITY

Directions: Record a concrete goal (results expected), specific deadline, and guidelines and parameters.

GOAL/ RESULTS	DEADLINE	GUIDELINES & PARAMETERS

No matter how small or large the goal of the assignment, be certain to include a very specific deadline. If the goal is a relatively long-term one, then break it down into smaller goals with intermediate deadlines.

Also, you may find it worthwhile to have the person you are managing construct an action plan. If so, be ready to lend a hand.

- First, review each smaller goal and its intermediate deadline.

- Then help the person make a list of the concrete actions required to achieve each smaller goal.

The following worksheet is a modified version of the "Plan of Action" tool provided in Chapter 7. It is tailored to your delegation role, and useful for breaking down a long-term goal into smaller goals and helping someone construct an action plan.

Use the next worksheet

to help someone else

make a plan of action.

Worksheet: DELEGATING EFFECTIVELY

For long-term goals, set smaller goals and deadlines.

LONG-TERM GOAL:

SMALLER GOALS	INTERMEDIATE DEADLINES
	➤

> WORKSHEET

To help someone make an action plan, take each smaller goal and intermediate deadline, and help the person make a list of all the concrete actions necessary to achieve each smaller goal.

SMALLER GOAL & DEADLINE	CONCRETE ACTIONS

MAKE SURE PEOPLE CAN MEET THEIR ASSIGNED GOALS

Every goal requires particular skills for its accomplishment; it also requires a certain amount of knowledge, wisdom, and experience. Thus you must be sure that the person you are managing has the skills, knowledge, wisdom, and experience necessary to achieve the goal you want to assign. If you need to bring that person up to speed on any or all of these four elements, use the next tool to brainstorm the fastest and most effective way to do so.

▶ Brainstorm

- **What is the person's assignment?**

- **What concrete actions does it involve?**

▶

> **Brainstorm**

- What skills, knowledge, wisdom, and experience does it require?

- Using the information above as a base, figure out the fastest and most effective way to bring this person up to speed.

◄ GUIDELINE 3 ►

MAKE SURE PEOPLE HAVE THE RESOURCES THEY NEED, AND ANTICIPATE OBSTACLES

Goals also require particular resources for their accomplishment; moreover, the path between setting a goal and meeting a goal is often fraught with obstacles. Consequently, you must be certain the person you are managing has the resources necessary to accomplish the goal you want to assign. Although you can't make the path to that accomplishment obstacle-free, you can try to anticipate the problems that may be encountered and provide a warning in advance.

The next tool will help you

keep to this guideline.

Worksheet: RESOURCES & OBSTACLES
Directions: Write down the assignment; then record the needed resources and likely obstacles to completing that assignment.
Assignment:

Necessary Resources	Likely Obstacles

COACH PEOPLE BY USING FAST FEEDBACK™

FAST Feedback™ is a system that encapsulates the best practices of the best coaching-style managers, based on continuing workplace-interview research conducted by RainmakerThinking. The key to *FAST Feedback™* is feedback itself—communicating with the people you manage in a way that is *directly responsive* to their words and actions. Giving regular feedback is the core competency of every good coaching-style manager.

FAST is an acronym that stands for:

> ➡ **FREQUENT**

> ➡ **ACCURATE**

> ➡ **SPECIFIC**

> ➡ **TIMELY**

These are the four best practices of the best coaching-style managers.

Frequent

Some people need feedback more often than others do—everyone has his or her own unique "feedback frequency." Moreover, different people need different amounts and different types of feedback, and these factors are likely to vary over time. In order to "tune in" to each person's unique frequency, think about each person you are managing and determine what kind of feedback he or she needs—how much, when, and in what form. Then try to provide the kind of feedback that works best for that person.

Accurate

The feedback you provide must be correct, balanced, and appropriate. Stop and check your facts before giving feedback. Overall, try to strike a good balance between praise and criticism. Most important, always choose your words carefully. You may even want to rehearse the feedback.

Specific

Feedback is not specific enough unless it points to concrete action steps. Every instance of feedback is also an opportunity to delegate—to assign concrete goals with specific deadlines and clear guidelines and parameters (see Guideline 1 above).

Timely

Always give feedback in a timely manner. The sooner the feedback follows the performance in question, the more impact the feedback will have. Giving immediate

---

Want to learn more about FAST Feedback™?

If so, check out the second edition of *FAST Feedback,* available from HRD Press. This handy pocket guide gives you the full basics along with helpful exercises, worksheets, and practice tips.

Also available: our full-scale training program, *FAST Feedback: Coaching Skills for Managers.*

For more information about these resources and our other programs and products from HRD Press, visit us at www.rainmakerthinking.com or give us a call at 203-772-2002.

---

feedback thus has the greatest impact. Keep in mind that timeliness requires time management skills.

Providing day-to-day coaching-style *FAST Feedback™* is the best way to keep the people you are managing focused, motivated, and moving in the right direction.

REWARD GOOD PERFORMANCE AND NOTHING ELSE

Make it very clear to everyone you manage exactly what performance you need and therefore will reward.

And try to reward people when they deliver results—no sooner, no later. Immediate rewards are the most effective because there can be no doubt about the reason for the rewards; this provides a greater sense of control and a higher level of reinforcement. Finally, remember that different people are motivated by different incentives; so when people perform, try to give them rewards they will value highly.

NEVER BE ABUSIVE

Never intimidate people. Never be mean to them. Never be abusive in any way. If criticism is unavoidable, make sure it's highly constructive, and always deliver it in a careful, respectful way. If you ever feel you are having trouble keeping to this guideline, immediately seek out a specialist who can help you.

ADOPT A TOTAL CUSTOMER SERVICE MINDSET

TO SUCCEED NOWADAYS, you need to treat everyone as a customer—co-workers, employees, managers, suppliers, service people, and actual customers. Never forget: No matter where you work, you are in business for yourself. Every unmet need is an opportunity to add value. Every untapped resource is waiting to be mined. If you don't know how to do something, learn. If you don't know how to get the job done, find a way.

These four guidelines will help:

1. **Identify opportunities to add value.**

2. **Sell your way into each challenge.**

3. **Close the deal.**

4. **Deliver, and always go the extra mile.**

IDENTIFY OPPORTUNITIES TO ADD VALUE

When you are looking for opportunities, remember that there are only five ways to add value:

1. Get lots of work done (complete tasks in a timely, competent manner or deliver a product or service).

2. Identify a problem that nobody has identified.

3. Solve a problem that nobody has solved.

4. Improve a service or product.

5. Invent a service or product.

SELL YOUR WAY INTO EACH CHALLENGE

Once you have identified an opportunity to add value, you need to sell your way into it. Remember three steps:

1. Define for yourself the value you want to add and are capable of adding; otherwise, it will be impossible to sell that value to anyone else.

2. Create an effective sales message to persuade decision-makers that the chance to add value should be pursued and that you are the right

person for the assignment. Your sales message should be brief, straightforward, and simple.

3. Be prepared to back up your sales message with a proposal answering the standard questions of *who, what, when, where, how,* and *why.* Make sure your proposal also answers these questions:

— *What's the benefit of what you're proposing?*

— *How can it be accomplished with minimum cost and little chance of anything going wrong?*

— *What resources will be needed, and where do you think they can be obtained?*

— *What are the potential problems, and what measures do you propose to avoid those problems?*

— *If the problems occur, how will you solve them?*

— *Overall, what role do you see for yourself in this proposal?*

— *What is the timeline for the proposal?*

CLOSE THE DEAL

You can sell and sell and sell, but it's all wasted time if you don't know how to close a deal. Be sure to take the following steps when you are trying to close a deal.

1. Know in advance your own desired terms (what you will ask for) and your own bottom line (the least favorable terms you are willing to accept).

2. Make sure you are talking to the person with the power to make the decision involved or at least influence the decision; otherwise you will be wasting your time.

3. Move the conversation to specific terms—time, place, and money.

4. State *your desired terms,* and then shut up. Stop talking. Be patient. Sit through the uncomfortable silence. Somebody has to talk first. The person who does is very likely to try to move toward the other person's negotiating position.

   So wait for your customer to say something. That something may be "Yes," or "No way," or "Maybe." You won't know which unless you listen carefully.

5. Stop and think about your response. If the customer has said, "Yes," then you just closed the deal. If customer has said, "Maybe," or has equivocated in any way, simply repeat *your desired terms* and shut up again. Keep doing this until you get to "Yes" or "No way." If the decision is "No way," go straight to the next step.

6. Ask the customer, "What do you need from me to close this deal?" Then, once again, listen carefully. If the other person's bottom line is lower than yours, you have nothing to lose because you are prepared to walk away. So go ahead and state *your own bottom line* and then shut up, stop talking, be patient—and listen carefully. If your customer's bottom line is higher than yours, accept your customer's bottom line terms: you just closed the deal.

7. When you close a deal, commit the terms to paper, initial the document, and pass it along to your customer for his or her initials. Do this even if you are working on a specific project with a co-worker or your boss or your best friend. Simply write a memo saying, "My understanding is that we agreed that we will work together on [specify]. You will do [specify] and I will do [specify] by next Thursday. Is this your understanding too?" Also, specify anything a third or fourth party will do.

Committing the terms to paper confirms that all the parties involved know what is expected of whom; this substantially reduces the chance for misunderstanding and conflict as everyone works together. From a legal standpoint, committing terms to paper and having both parties sign the

paper is proof that you have made an enforceable agreement, otherwise known as a contract.
In order to have an enforceable contract, you
need to include the following details:

— *What are you promising to do?*

— *What is the other person promising to do?*

— *By what date and time is each person's
performance promised, and in what place?*

Consider role-playing this entire process with a friend
or colleague. Agree on a hypothetical transaction and
hypothetical roles; then, take some time so each of you
can decide privately on ideal terms and a bottom line.
Finally, role-play the negotiation.

Note: Take turns being the "awesome negotiator," or
your role play could stall at the fourth step.

GUIDELINE 4

DELIVER, AND ALWAYS GO THE EXTRA MILE

After you close the deal, you'd better be prepared to
deliver and try to go the extra mile. Always go one step
beyond the specifications: add the bells and whistles
and tie a bow on it. Get it done early; and when payment
time comes, discount the price. The best approach is to
always under-promise and over-deliver.

Keep in mind these six simple rules of customer service:

1. Listen much more than you talk.

2. Never put your desires ahead of your customer's needs.

3. Convey honesty and accuracy in everything you do, no matter how minuscule the work may seem.

4. Never say, "I can't help you."

5. Always be on time.

6. Always provide follow-up service. Ask your customer if he or she was satisfied with the results of your work. Ask if there is anything else your customer would like you to do. If there was any problem with the work you did, offer to do whatever is necessary to make it right.

SUCCESS HAPPENS ONE MOMENT AT A TIME

THE ONLY WAY TO SUCCEED is one moment at a time. Long-term success is simply the accumulation of many, many, many successful moments. Every single moment counts. The question I want to leave you with is this: *What are you going to do right now to contribute to your success?*

In this final chapter, you'll find the tools to help you make every moment count, starting *RIGHT NOW.* There are five main steps to follow:

1. **Revisit your one-year goals, and commit to them.**

2. **Set intermediate goals and deadlines.**

3. **Review the goals for this month, and set weekly goals.**

4. **See what action steps you need to take this week.**

5. **Decide which action steps you are going to take right away.**

Let's take a closer look.

 # REVISIT YOUR ONE-YEAR GOALS, AND COMMIT TO THEM

Return to the process you began in Chapter 2 (see the worksheet "Setting Goals for Success"). You created a vision of your future, and you set goals for next year in four areas:

1. Learning
2. Relationships
3. Adding value
4. Moving your life toward greater balance

Take a moment now to revisit those goals—think about the goals you set and refine them as necessary until you really believe in them. Record the refined goals on the next page.

Make a commitment to these goals. Right now, tell yourself: "I am going to achieve these goals over the next twelve months."

Refining Your One-Year Goals

LEARNING:

RELATIONSHIPS:

ADDING VALUE:

MOVING TOWARD GREATER BALANCE:

 ## SET INTERMEDIATE GOALS AND DEADLINES

Now make a plan. Map out all the intermediate goals and deadlines along the way to each goal. If you are going to achieve your one-year goals, what must you achieve by the eleven-month mark? Ten? Nine, eight, seven, six, five, four, three, two, and one? Spend time mapping out all the intermediate goals and deadlines to keep you on track toward your one-year goals.

The following planning sheet

will help you with this step.

Planning Sheet: ONE-YEAR GOALS

	Learning	Relationships	Adding Value	Balance
One-Year Goals				
Within 11 Months				
Within 10 Months				
Within 9 Months				
Within 8 Months				
Within 7 Months				

▶ Planning Sheet: ONE-YEAR GOALS

	Learning	Relationships	Adding Value	Balance
Within 6 Months				
Within 5 Months				
Within 4 Months				
Within 3 Months				
Within 2 Months				
THIS MONTH				

REVIEW THE GOALS FOR THIS MONTH, AND SET WEEKLY GOALS

Look at which intermediate goals you need to accomplish in the coming month. Organize those goals into weekly goals.

The next planning sheet, "This Month's Goals," will help you with this step.

Be sure to complete your planning sheet

before going on to Step 4.

SEE WHAT ACTION STEPS YOU NEED TO TAKE THIS WEEK

Focus on your goals for the end of this week. What concrete action steps will you need to take this week to accomplish your goals?

Record those action steps on the planning sheet "This Week's Action Steps," on page 134.

Be sure to complete your planning sheet

before going on to Step 5.

Planning Sheet: THIS MONTH'S GOALS				
	Learning	Relationships	Adding Value	Balance
By End of Month **Date:**				
Within 3 Weeks **Date:**				
Within 2 Weeks **Date:**				
By End of This Week **Date:**				

Planning Sheet: THIS WEEK'S ACTION STEPS				
	Learning	Relationships	Adding Value	Balance
ACTION STEPS				

DECIDE WHICH ACTION STEPS YOU ARE GOING TO TAKE RIGHT AWAY

What must be done first? What must be done tomorrow—or better yet, TODAY? Make a list.

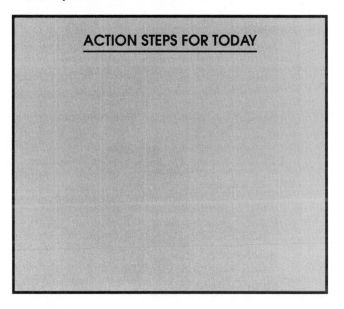

ACTION STEPS FOR TODAY

Now choose one—just one—action step and GO DO IT RIGHT NOW. Get yourself on the path to success without delay. Learn, build relationships, add value, and move toward greater balance. Again, the only way to succeed is one moment at a time. Make this moment count, and every moment count, from now on.